CONNECT

A TIMELINE OF PRESIDENTIAL ELECTIONS

by Barbara Krasner

Consultant:
Christina Wolbrecht
Associate Professor of Political Science
University of Notre Dame

CAPSTONE PRESS
a capstone imprint

Connect is published by Capstone Press,
1710 Roe Crest Drive, North Mankato, Minnesota 56003
www.capstonepub.com

Library of Congress Cataloging-in-Publication Data
Krasner, Barbara, author.
   A Timeline of Presidential Elections/by Barbara Krasner.
          pages cm.—(Connect. Presidential Politics)
   Summary: "Offers a chronological look at U.S. presidential elections utilizing an
info graphic approach"—Provided by publisher.
   Includes bibliographical references and index.
   Audience: Age 8–14.
   Audience: Grades 4 to 6.
   ISBN 978-1-4914-8239-1 (library binding)
   ISBN 978-1-4914-8629-0 (paperback)
   ISBN 978-1-4914-8650-4 (ebook PDF)
1. Presidents—United States—Election—Juvenile literature. I. Title.
   JK524.K69 2016
   324.973—dc23   2015032273

Editorial Credits
Jennifer Huston, editor; Veronica Scott, designer; Tracy Cummins, media researcher;
Kathy McColley, production specialist

Photo Credits
Alamy: Bygone Collection, 22 Top, Everett Collection, 33 Bottom, Niday Picture
Library, 20; Capstone Press, 8, 10 Bottom, 12, 19, Jennifer Huston, 45 Bottom, Karon
Dubke, 27 Bottom, 33 Middle; Corbis: Bettmann, 37 Bottom, 40 Top, Hulton-Deutsch,
29 Bottom, REUTERS/Mike Segar, 43 Bottom; Getty Images: CBS Photo Archive,
35 Bottom, Gamma-Keystone, 39 Top, JP Jazz Archive/Redferns, 26, Newsmakers, 38,
TIM CLARY/AFP, 41 Top, Underwood Archives, 27 Top Right, 32, Universal History
Archive/UIG, 18; Courtesy of James Madison's Montpelier: 9 Bottom; Library of
Congress: Front Cover Top, 6, 7 Left, 7 Right, 9 Top Middle, 10 Right, 14 Top,
14 Bottom, 17 Top, 17 Middle, 17 Bottom, 22 Bottom, 25, Carol M. Highsmith Archive,
13 Top, Harris & Ewing, 27 Top Left, U.S. Army A.A.F. photo, 31; Newscom: Dennis
Brack, 39 Bottom, Everett Collection, 15 Top, 23, Everett Collection/CSU Archives,
29 Top, 34, 35 Top, 37 Top, Jose Giribas Ropi/ZUMA Press, 40 Bottom; NOAA: 16;
Shutterstock: Dan Howell, 42, Everett Historical, 21, 24, 28, Jacob Hamblin, 11 Left,
javarman, Design Element, Matt Trommer, 15 Bottom, NatBasil, Design Element,
watcharakun, Design Element, Zffoto, 30 Top; Thinkstock: Chip Somodevilla, Front
Cover Bottom, Junko Kimura/Getty Images, 44 Bottom; Wikimedia: 10 Left, 11 Right,
13 Bottom, 43 Middle, defenseimagery.mil, 40 Middle, DoD photo by Senior Master
Sgt. Thomas Meneguin/U.S. Air Force, 44–45, Gerald R. Ford Presidential Library, 36,
Google Art Project, 9 Top Right, NARA, 30 Bottom, 33 Top, 35 Middle, Quartermaster,
41 Bottom, The White House Historical Association, 9 Top Left, White House photo
by Eric Draper, 43 Top

Printed in the United States of America in North Mankato, Minnesota.
009221CGS16

TABLE OF CONTENTS

INTRODUCTION

Nearly four years after the Revolutionary War ended, the United States still didn't have a leader. At the **Constitutional Convention of 1787**, state representatives agreed that someone needed to run the country. They discussed how to elect this person and what powers he should have.

Members of the convention met from May to September. In the end they came up with a procedure for selecting a president: the Electoral College. Each state chooses **electors** equal in number to their representatives and senators combined. For example, if a state has two U.S. senators and five U.S. representatives, it gets seven electoral votes. When citizens vote for the person they want to be president, their votes are the popular vote. But the popular vote does not directly determine who becomes president. The Electoral College does that. When a candidate wins the popular vote in a state, that state's electors cast their electoral votes for that candidate. Whoever receives a majority (more than 50 percent) of the electoral votes becomes president. If nobody receives a majority or in the case of a tie, the House of Representatives decides the winner.

Originally the runner-up became vice president. That changed with the 12th **Amendment** in 1804, which required electors to cast separate votes for president and vice president. In the 1860s, political parties began pairing up presidential and vice presidential candidates to run on the ballot together. It would be more than 100 years before presidential candidates were able to choose their own vice presidential candidates.

Constitutional Convention of 1787—a gathering in which representatives of the United States developed laws by which the new country would govern itself
electors—people who vote to choose between candidates running for office
amendment—a change made to a law or a legal document
resign—to voluntarily give up a job, position, or office

On some occasions, elections are not necessary. When a president dies in office, the vice president automatically becomes commander in chief. The vice president serves until the next regularly scheduled election and can then run for president if he desires. Eight U.S. presidents have either died of natural causes or were killed while in office. One **resigned**.

Election campaigns and issues represent the very history of the United States. This book presents America's election history from the first president, George Washington, to Barack Obama, the 44th president.

Political Parties in the United States

A political party is a group of people with common beliefs and goals that they seek to achieve through laws. The dominant parties have changed over time, and some have died out. Here is a brief history of political parties in the United States and what they stand for:

Party	Years Active	Beliefs/Goals
Federalists	1792-1824	favored a strong federal government
Democratic-Republicans	1792-1825	favored strong state governments
Democrats	1828-present	currently believe the government should help take care of individuals; support civil rights and programs to help the poor
Whigs	1833-1854	believed Congress should be stronger than the president; supported taxes to promote industry
Republicans	1854-present	currently more conservative socially and economically; believe everyone is responsible for themselves and government should play a limited role

CHAPTER 1

A NEW NATION STEPS FORWARD
(1789-1828)

After the Revolutionary War (1775–1783), George Washington was happy to return to Mount Vernon, his Virginia plantation. He was incredibly popular, and some people wanted him to be their new leader. But Washington wasn't thrilled with the idea. However, when electors **unanimously** chose him to be the country's first president, he felt it was his patriotic duty.

- - - - - 1789 - - - - -

Each elector casts two votes for president. All 69 electors vote for Federalist George Washington, former commander in chief of the Continental army. He becomes America's first president and is the only one elected by unanimous vote. John Adams, who receives 34 votes, becomes vice president.

- - - - - 1792 - - - - -

Washington is elected to a second term as president. John Adams comes in second again and continues as vice president. Washington's **inauguration** speech contains only 135 words. It is the shortest one on record.

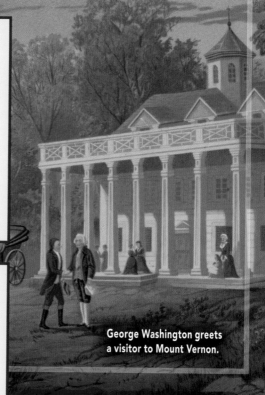

George Washington greets a visitor to Mount Vernon.

unanimously—agreed on by everyone
inauguration—a formal ceremony to swear a person into political office

1796

Washington refuses to run for a third term. He fears that serving for too long would give a leader too much power. Federalist John Adams wins the presidential election against Democratic-Republican Thomas Jefferson. Adams wins by just three electoral votes. As the runner-up, Jefferson becomes vice president. This is the first and only time the president and vice president belong to different political parties.

1800

Adams and Jefferson oppose each other in a bitter fight. Adams receives only 65 electoral votes. Jefferson and Aaron Burr each receive 73. But during the campaign it is assumed that Burr is running for vice president. However, he refuses to step down. Because Jefferson and Burr receive the same number of electoral votes, the House of Representatives must break the tie. It takes 36 rounds of voting before Jefferson is named the winner.

Frenemies John Adams and Thomas Jefferson

Friends John Adams and Thomas Jefferson worked side by side for America's independence. But when Jefferson defeated Adams in the election of 1800, they became bitter opponents. After Jefferson retired in 1809, they renewed their friendship. The two great leaders died within five hours of each other on July 4, 1826, the 50th anniversary of the signing of the Declaration of Independence.

Thomas Jefferson

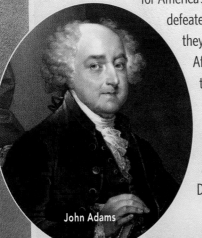

John Adams

7

1804

With the adoption of the 12th Amendment to the Constitution, electors must cast one vote for president and one for vice president. This reduces the chances that the president and vice president come from different political parties. Thomas Jefferson easily wins a second term as president over Federalist candidate Charles Pinckney. Economic prosperity and Jefferson's Louisiana Purchase in 1803 make him a popular choice for president.

The Louisiana Purchase

During his first term in office, Thomas Jefferson bought the Louisiana Territory from France. For $15 million (about $319 million today), the young United States doubled its size. The deal included New Orleans and 828,000 square miles (2,144,510 square kilometers) of land to the north and west. This large area included land that would eventually become all or part of 15 states. These are Arkansas, Colorado, Iowa, Kansas, Louisiana, Minnesota, Missouri, Montana, Nebraska, New Mexico, North Dakota, Oklahoma, South Dakota, Texas, and Wyoming. America had a new western border, and expansion became a presidential priority.

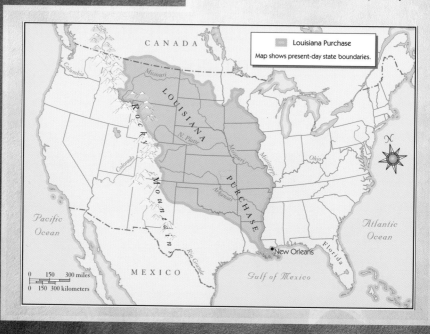

Louisiana Purchase

Map shows present-day state boundaries.

- - - - - 1808 - - - - -

U.S. Secretary of State James Madison is elected president. He is a cousin of future president Zachary Taylor and a distant cousin of George Washington.

From left to right: James Madison, Zachary Taylor, George Washington

- - - - - 1812 - - - - -

With America at war with Britain again, Madison beats Federalist DeWitt Clinton to win a second term in office. When British troops arrive in Maryland in 1814, Madison joins American troops fighting the British there. His wife, Dolley, remains at the White House until the British are just hours away. When she finally leaves, she takes a painting of George Washington and a copy of the Declaration of Independence. Soon after she flees, the British burn the White House and the Capitol building.

Dolley Madison instructs servants to take down a painting of George Washington so the British cannot destroy it.

- - - - - 1816 - - - - -

Madison does not seek re-election for a third term. James Monroe, who served as Madison's secretary of state, runs for president on the Democratic-Republican ticket. Monroe defeats Federalist candidate Rufus King in a landslide, 183 electoral votes to 34.

- - - - - 1820 - - - - -

Monroe's party, the Democratic-Republicans, is so sure he'll win that they do not bother to formally **nominate** him. Even so, he receives all but one electoral vote against John Quincy Adams, son of America's second president.

James Monroe

- - - - - 1824 - - - - -

Due to fighting within the party, four different candidates run for president on the Democratic-Republican ticket, including Andrew Jackson and John Quincy Adams. Charismatic war hero Jackson wins the popular vote. However, none of the candidates earns the required majority of electoral votes (131). So, according to the Constitution, the House of Representatives gets to decide who will be president. They choose John Quincy Adams.

Andrew Jackson

The "Corrupt Bargain"

Some people believed that John Quincy Adams struck a deal with Speaker of the House Henry Clay. If Adams won, he'd make Clay his secretary of state. Believers of this "corrupt bargain" theory think that Clay convinced members of the House to elect Adams over Jackson.

Electoral College results, 1824

House of Representatives vote, 1825

Andrew Jackson battles John Quincy Adams again. This time, Jackson wins with more than twice as many electoral votes as Adams. Jackson leads the new Democratic Party, which evolves from Jefferson's Democratic-Republicans. Today the Democratic Party is the oldest existing political party in the United States.

John Quincy Adams

nominate—to suggest that someone would be the right person to do a job

CHAPTER 2

WESTERN EXPANSION
(1832–1856)

As the nation expanded, so did its political party system. The Whig and Democratic parties eventually replaced the Federalist and Democratic-Republican parties.

Expansion demanded resources to develop land and build canals and railroads. Banks did not always have these resources, which caused financial panics in 1819, 1837, and 1857.

Expansion also created a conflict with Mexico. As part of the treaty that ended the Mexican War (1846–1848), the United States gained a large amount of new territory. As a result, the nation stretched from the Atlantic Ocean to the Pacific Ocean.

As new states formed, politicians argued over whether slavery should be permitted within them. By the 1850s this became the most argued election issue.

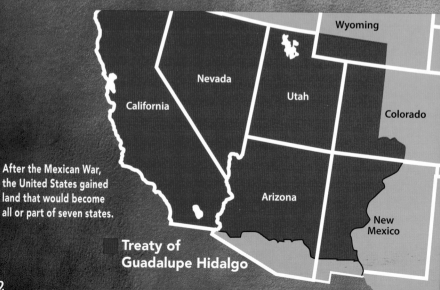

Wyoming

Nevada

Utah

California

Colorado

After the Mexican War, the United States gained land that would become all or part of seven states.

Arizona

New Mexico

Treaty of
Guadalupe Hidalgo

Political Party Conventions

1832

With great support from the South and West, "Old Hickory" Andrew Jackson wins re-election against Whig candidate Henry Clay. This is the first presidential election in which candidates were nominated at a national party convention.

In the nation's early days, members of Congress nominated presidential candidates. But over time, the citizens wanted more decision-making power over the nominations. That's when the political convention was born. The original purpose of political conventions was to nominate the party's presidential candidate.

Today presidential candidates are chosen through the **primary** election process. During the primaries, citizens vote for who they would like to see nominated for president. Typically, the candidate who gets the most votes in the primaries formally accepts the nomination during the party's convention.

1836

Planning to retire, Jackson handpicks his successor—his vice president, Martin Van Buren. The Whig Party selects four different candidates, including William Henry Harrison and Daniel Webster. The Whigs hope one of the four will defeat Van Buren or that the House will have to choose the winner. The plan backfires and Van Buren wins by 97 electoral votes. Van Buren is the first president not born under British rule.

1840

Van Buren and Harrison run against each other once again. This time Harrison wins by a landslide. At age 68, Harrison is the oldest person sworn in as president until Ronald Reagan in 1981. However, his time as commander in chief is very brief. He dies from **pneumonia** just a month after taking the oath of office. Vice President John Tyler steps in as president.

William Her Harrison

primary—an election in which candidates of the same party try to win the party's nomination as candidate for a particular office
pneumonia—a serious disease that causes the lungs to fill with fluid

1844

Slavery is a major issue during this campaign. Tyler does not make a bid for re-election. Instead, he supports the nomination of Tennessee's Democratic governor, James K. Polk. Although Polk and his opponent Henry Clay own slaves, both oppose slavery. Polk supports western expansion of the nation while Clay rejects it. At age 49, Polk is the youngest man to be elected president at the time.

1848

For the first time in American history, voting for president occurs nationwide on the same day. Whig candidate and Mexican War hero Zachary Taylor beats Democrat Lewis Cass. But when Taylor dies on July 9, 1850, Vice President Millard Fillmore takes over as president.

1852

Fillmore seeks re-election, but he does not receive the Whig Party's nomination. Instead, the Whigs choose Winfield Scott, former commander of U.S. forces in the Mexican War. The Democratic Party nominates Franklin Pierce. They use the campaign slogan, "We Polked You in 1844. We shall Pierce You in 1852." Pierce defeats Scott by a whopping 254 electoral votes out of 296. Scott is the Whigs' final candidate. The party breaks up because its members disagree over slavery.

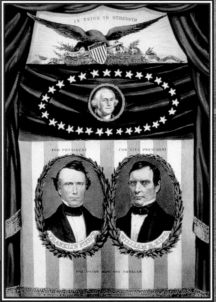

1856

The breakup of the Whig Party opens up other possibilities. Former President Millard Fillmore represents the new "Know-Nothing" party but barely gets any electoral votes. The new Republican Party chooses John C. Fremont as its first presidential candidate. But even Fremont's father-in-law, a Missouri senator, backs Democrat James Buchanan. Buchanan easily defeats Fremont.

The Birth of the Republican Party

In 1854, a group of former Whigs met in Ripon, Wisconsin, to discuss creating a new political party. They believed in putting the interests of the nation as a whole above those of the individual states. They were also fiercely opposed to slavery. They called themselves the Republican Party.

CHAPTER 3

CIVIL WAR AND RECONSTRUCTION (1860–1876)

Slavery divided the nation. In 1861, southern states began **seceding** from the Union. They went on to form the Confederate States of America with Jefferson Davis as their president. When war broke out between the states, Abraham Lincoln devoted his presidency to restoring the Union.

After the war, rebuilding the South became a presidential priority. It also opened the door for **corruption** and **profiteering**. This period, known as Reconstruction, brought the southern states back into the Union. In 1870 the 15th Amendment gave African-Americans the right to vote. However, they often had to risk their lives to do so.

States that seceded before April 15, 1861
States that seceded after April 15, 1861
Union states that permitted slavery
Union states that forbade slavery
Territories, unaffiliated

1860

Republican Abraham Lincoln and Democrat Stephen A. Douglas face off in the presidential election. Lincoln sweeps the North and wins with 180 of 303 electoral votes. Lincoln receives 108 votes more than his nearest opponent, John C. Breckinridge. Although Douglas comes in second in the popular vote, he finishes last in the electoral vote.

Unhappy with Lincoln's victory, South Carolina secedes from the Union in December. Over time, 10 more states follow, forming the Confederate States of America. The Civil War breaks out in April 1861. In what was called the War Between the States, brothers fought brothers and fathers fought sons in the battle over slavery.

Abraham Lincoln (left) and Hannibal Hamlin (right) won the election of 1860.

1864

Lincoln seeks re-election, but his own general, Democrat George B. McClellan, runs against him. McClellan wants to stop the war and is considered a favorite. But a string of Union victories helps keep Lincoln in office. He wins by an overwhelming 191 electoral votes. However, on April 14, 1865, John Wilkes Booth shoots Lincoln at Ford's Theatre in Washington, D.C. When Lincoln dies the following day, Vice President Andrew Johnson steps in.

secede—to formally withdraw from a group or an organization
corruption—doing things that are wrong or illegal to get money, favors, or power
profiteer—to make money by selling goods that are in short supply

As a general in the Union army, Ulysses S. Grant was a war hero. But his years as president were marked by corruption and an economic depression.

- - - - - 1868 - - - - -

On February 24, 1868, Congress votes to **impeach** Johnson for "high crimes and misdemeanors." One of these crimes includes allegedly violating an act Congress had passed. The impeachment is never carried out, but Johnson is not allowed to seek re-election. Instead, Republicans nominate Union war hero Ulysses S. Grant. Grant wins easily against Democrat Horatio Seymour.

impeach—to bring formal charges against a public official who may have committed a crime while in office

1872

Grant wins re-election even though his administration is accused of stealing federal funds and accepting bribes from railroad companies. One of his opponents, Horace Greeley, encourages westward expansion with the slogan, "Go West, young man, and grow up with the country." However, Greeley dies a few weeks after the general election, before the electoral votes are counted. He is the only candidate ever to do so.

1876

Grant wants to run for a third term, but his party advises against it. Rutherford B. Hayes eventually wins the support of the Republican Party. Hayes and Democrat Samuel Tilden both promise to end the corruption that has marked Grant's administration. Tilden wins the popular election by nearly 300,000 votes. But Republicans question the validity of 20 electoral votes. Through a special committee of Congress, Hayes wins by one electoral vote.

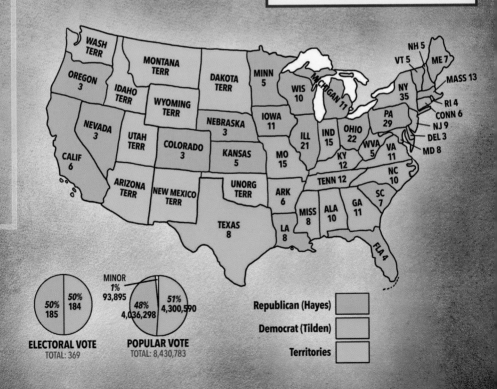

ELECTORAL VOTE
TOTAL: 369

50% 185 | 50% 184

POPULAR VOTE
TOTAL: 8,430,783

MINOR 1% 93,895
48% 4,036,298 | 51% 4,300,590

Republican (Hayes)
Democrat (Tilden)
Territories

CHAPTER 4

THE GILDED AGE AND THE PROGRESSIVE ERA (1880-1912)

The United States became less agricultural and more industrial in the late 1800s. People increasingly worked in factories and offices in cities instead of on farms and in small towns. Along with this shift in the economy came new forms of corruption and greed. The rich grew richer as railroads and wealthy people with wild moneymaking schemes controlled the economy. Writer Mark Twain referred to this period as "the Gilded Age."

Some activists, known as Progressives, wanted to eliminate political corruption and break up business **monopolies**. They wanted to improve unhealthy living and working conditions.

At the end of the 19th century, America prospered. After the Spanish-American War (1898), the United States gained new territories, including the Philippines, Puerto Rico, and Guam. But in 1914, the **assassination** of Archduke Franz Ferdinand of the Austro-Hungarian Empire brought war to Europe and tough choices to America's leaders.

1880

With Hayes choosing not to seek a second term in office, the Republicans nominate James Garfield over former president Ulysses S. Grant. The Democrats choose Union war hero Winfield Hancock. Garfield wins with 214 of 369 electoral votes.

On July 2, 1881, Charles Guiteau shoots Garfield in Washington, D.C. Doctors are unable to remove the bullet, and Garfield suffers for more than two months. During this time, the country runs without a president. His situation raises questions about what happens when a president is still alive but cannot perform the duties of the office. When Garfield dies on September 19, Vice President Chester Arthur takes over.

The 25th Amendment

Before Congress passed the 25th Amendment in 1967, there was no official rule for who takes over if a president dies, resigns, or cannot perform his duties. According to the 25th Amendment, if the president dies or resigns, the vice president takes over as president. If the president is unable to perform his duties, the vice president becomes "acting president." The vice president returns to his role as second in command when the president resumes his duties.

This amendment also set rules for what to do if the office of the vice president is left empty. Prior to this, if the vice president died, resigned, or took over the president's duties, nobody filled in. The 25th Amendment gave the president the power to nominate a new vice president.

1884

Arthur's bid for re-election is crushed when Republicans nominate third-time presidential hopeful, James Blaine, Garfield's secretary of state. The Democrats nominate New York Governor Grover Cleveland. Campaigns erupt into personal attacks. With support from New York, Cleveland defeats Blaine.

monopoly—a situation in which a supplier can control the price of a good or service because it is the only supplier
assassination—the murder of someone who is well known or important

- - - - - 1888 - - - - -

"Grandfather's hat fits!" is the campaign slogan for Republican candidate Benjamin Harrison, grandson of ninth president, William Henry Harrison. **Incumbent** Cleveland wins the popular vote by a narrow margin (49 percent to Harrison's 48 percent). However, the states Harrison won have more electoral votes, so he slides into victory.

- - - - - 1892 - - - - -

Harrison and Cleveland square off in a rematch. This time Cleveland wins with more than 62 percent of the electoral vote. He also earns the distinction of being both the 22nd and 24th president. He is the only president to serve two **nonconsecutive** terms.

- - - - - 1896 - - - - -

Cleveland does not seek another term. Republican candidate William McKinley's campaign manager distributes pamphlets in different languages to appeal to immigrant voters. Democratic candidate William Jennings Bryan's support from farmers is no match for McKinley's from big business and immigrants.

A campaign poster for William McKinley illustrates his promise to return prosperity to a nation that had been in an economic depression for several years.

In 1901 President McKinley was shot while attending a world's fair in Buffalo, New York. The fair showcased new inventions, such as the X-ray machine. However, doctors refused to use the X-ray machine on the president because they were unsure of its side effects. Had they used it, they might have been able to remove the bullet and save his life.

- - - - - 1900 - - - - -

Republicans nominate McKinley for a second term with New York Governor and Spanish-American War hero Theodore Roosevelt as his **running mate**. The election pits McKinley against Bryan for a second time. With the energetic Roosevelt campaigning, McKinley wins easily with 65 percent of the electoral vote.

On September 6, 1901, Leon Czolgosz shoots McKinley in Buffalo, New York. McKinley dies on September 14, and Theodore Roosevelt becomes president.

incumbent—the person currently in office
nonconsecutive—with a gap between; not one after the other
running mate—the person a candidate is running with

----- 1904 -----

Although Roosevelt does not always see eye to eye with some more traditional Republicans, they nominate him for president. Roosevelt beats his opponent, Democrat Alton B. Parker, in a landslide with 336 of 476 electoral votes. Now that he has won an election on his own, he tells his wife, "I am no longer a political accident."

----- 1908 -----

Roosevelt decides not to run in 1908 even though he feels he still has much to accomplish. Instead, he backs Republican nominee and Secretary of War William Howard Taft. Taft runs against Bryan, who is making his third bid for the presidency. With support from the popular Roosevelt, Taft wins easily with nearly twice as many electoral votes as Bryan.

Theodore Roosevelt was a sickly child who battled asthma and other illnesses. Some relatives thought he wouldn't make it to adulthood, but by age 42, he was president of the United States.

- - - - - 1912 - - - - -

Dissatisfied with Taft's performance as president, Roosevelt decides to run again. But when the Republicans nominate Taft a second time, Roosevelt forms his own party, the Progressives. The Progressives are popularly known as the Bull Moose Party, after a phrase Roosevelt used to describe himself. They believe in giving women the right to vote, setting a minimum wage, and establishing an eight-hour workday. The Democrats nominate New Jersey Governor Woodrow Wilson. Wilson wins easily with 435 electoral votes to Roosevelt's 88 and Taft's 8. This election marks the first time all 48 continental states participate. Two years later, when World War I breaks out in Europe, Wilson vows to keep the United States out of the conflict.

Theodore Roosevelt (left) backed William Howard Taft (right) for president in 1908. But when Roosevelt decided to run for president again in 1912, the two opposed each other.

25

CHAPTER 5

THE GREAT WAR AND THE JAZZ AGE (1916-1924)

Despite Wilson's desire to remain **neutral**, the United States entered the war in 1917. After World War I ended in November 1918, Wilson played an important role in creating the Treaty of Versailles in 1919. Included in that peace treaty were Wilson's plans for the League of Nations. The League was an organization made up of countries whose goal was to maintain peace. Ironically, the United States never joined.

In the United States, "the Roaring Twenties" and "the Jazz Age" were periods of economic boom. In 1919 the 18th Amendment made the manufacture and sale of alcohol illegal. This was known as Prohibition. The decade was characterized by illegal drinking establishments known as **speakeasies** and by over-eager financial investments. New immigration laws severely restricted newcomers. With the passage of the 19th Amendment in 1920, women finally gained the right to vote.

Bands such as King Oliver's Creole Jazz Band became wildly popular in the 1920s.

neutral—not taking any side in a war
speakeasy—a place that illegally sells alcoholic drinks

----- 1916 -----

The Democrats continue to support Wilson and his desire to stay out of World War I. The Republicans push for war and nominate Charles Hughes. Newspapers forecast a Republican victory, but California's electoral votes push Wilson over the top. After Germany attacks passenger and merchant ships, the United States enters the war in 1917. When Wilson suffers a stroke in 1919, his wife, Edith, unofficially takes over his duties until the end of his term.

A Hard-Won Battle for the Female Vote

For nearly a century, many American women had been working to gain the right to vote. In August 1920, the 19th Amendment to the U.S. Constitution became law. For many women, the election of 1920 was the first time they could legally vote.

----- 1920 -----

Due to his failing health, Wilson doesn't seek a third term. Democratic nominee James Cox campaigns for peace and membership in the League of Nations. Even so, the war-weary nation elects Republican Senator Warren G. Harding. With his "Return to Normalcy" campaign, Harding easily wins with 404 electoral votes to Cox's 127. On August 2, 1923, Harding dies of a heart attack. Vice President Calvin Coolidge is sworn into office.

----- 1924 -----

In just over a year as president, Coolidge has restored America's confidence in the government. Americans decide to "Keep Cool with Cal." He easily wins the nomination at the Republican convention, which is broadcast on the radio for the first time. He faces off against Democrat John Davis and Progressive Robert LaFollette. Coolidge comes out on top. This is the first election in which American Indians have the right to vote in a presidential election.

KEEP COOL WITH CAL
COOLIDGE FOR PRESIDENT

CHAPTER 6

THE GREAT DEPRESSION AND WORLD WAR II
(1928-1944)

Herbert Hoover's presidency started on a hopeful note, but by January 1931, 5 million Americans were out of work. They blamed Hoover for their hardships. Hoover's initial optimism gave way to helplessness.

Franklin Delano Roosevelt promised Americans a "new deal." Beginning with his first day in office, Roosevelt kept his promise. He introduced new government programs to address America's economic problems. Later that year, Prohibition was **repealed**. The United States ultimately climbed out of the Great Depression by entering World War II.

Workers build a dam in Tennessee in 1942. The project was one of Roosevelt's New Deal programs.

repeal—to officially cancel something, such as a law
polio—a disease affecting the nerves, spinal cord, and brain

- - - - 1928 - - - - -

With Coolidge choosing not to run for re-election, U.S. Secretary of Commerce Herbert Hoover wins the Republican nomination. Democrats choose New York Governor Al Smith, the first Roman Catholic presidential candidate. Promising to continue the economic boom the nation has experienced under Coolidge, Hoover wins in a landslide. He receives 444 electoral votes to Smith's 44. The economic boom comes to a halt when the stock market crashes on October 29, 1929. Although Hoover reassures the country that better times are just around the corner, America plunges into the Great Depression.

- - - - 1932 - - - - -

Despite being confined to a wheelchair because of **polio**, Democrat Franklin Delano Roosevelt (FDR) accepts his party's nomination in person. He is the first presidential candidate to do so. With promises of "a new deal for the American people," Roosevelt easily defeats Hoover. He wins 42 of 48 states.

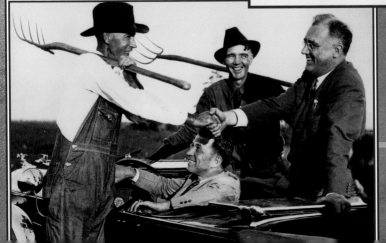

FDR meets some farmers while on the campaign trail in Georgia in 1932.

1936

Roosevelt is easily re-elected for a second term. His opponent, Kansas Governor Alfred M. Landon, suffers one of the worst defeats in presidential election history. He receives only 8 electoral votes compared to Roosevelt's 523. The inauguration date officially moves from March to January.

8

523

The USS *Arizona* burns after the Japanese attack Pearl Harbor. The wreck of the battleship remains at the bottom of Pearl Harbor and is visible from the USS *Arizona* memorial.

1940

Newspapers back Republican Wendell L. Willkie, but most others still support Roosevelt. The incumbent vows to keep the United States out of World War II, which started in 1939. He is re-elected with nearly 85 percent of the electoral vote. He becomes the first and only president elected more than twice. Japanese forces attack American ships at Pearl Harbor in Hawaii on December 7, 1941. The next day, the United States enters World War II.

A mushroom cloud erupts following the dropping of an atomic bomb over Nagasaki, Japan, on August 9, 1945.

- - - - - 1944 - - - - -

Despite Roosevelt's failing health, Democrats support him for a fourth term. He beats Republican Thomas Dewey with 432 electoral votes to Dewey's 99. When Roosevelt dies on April 12, 1945, Vice President Harry S. Truman assumes the presidency. In August, Truman decides to drop atomic bombs on Japan, ending World War II.

CHAPTER 7

POSTWAR AMERICA (1948-1956)

The United States emerged from World War II as a **superpower**. As fear of **communism** spread, the nation entered a **Cold War** with the Soviet Union.

Europe demanded America's attention too. Many countries were devastated by the war. Thousands were left homeless and starving. The United States offered food, medicine, and other economic aid.

1948

The Democratic Party wants the popular General Dwight D. Eisenhower to run for president. But he declines the nomination. Instead Democrats back President Truman. He campaigns widely, giving 300 speeches to 6 million people. On the night of the election, the *Chicago Daily Tribune* incorrectly reports that the Republican candidate, New York Governor Thomas E. Dewey, has won. However, Truman wins the popular vote as well as the majority of electoral votes in 28 states for an easy victory.

Harry Truman displays a newspaper incorrectly reporting that he lost the election.

superpower—an extremely powerful nation
communism—a way of running a country in which the government owns almost everything
Cold War—a conflict between the United States and the Soviet Union; although there was no direct fighting, the conflict lasted from about 1947 to 1990

- - - - - 1952 - - - - -

Truman loses popularity over the Korean War (1950–1953) and does not seek re-election. This time, Dwight D. Eisenhower accepts the Republican nomination. He faces off against Democrat Adlai Stevenson. Eisenhower vows to end the war in Korea. His campaign offers the slogan "I Like Ike" on buttons, stockings, and jewelry, among other things. Eisenhower wins with 442 electoral votes to Stevenson's 89. On July 27, 1953, the Korean War comes to an end.

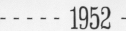

PEACE · PROGRESS · PROSPERITY
I LIKE IKE

Five-star General Dwight D. Eisenhower (left) served as supreme commander of the Allied forces in Europe during World War II.

- - - - - 1956 - - - - -

Eisenhower and Stevenson face off in a rematch of the 1952 election. With a prosperous economy and the end of the Korean War, Eisenhower and running mate Richard M. Nixon are easily re-elected.

Eisenhower (left) and his running mate—a young senator from California named Richard Nixon

CHAPTER 8

THE VIETNAM ERA
(1960-1976)

The 1960s and 1970s were troublesome times. The Cold War heated up, forcing President Kennedy to make difficult decisions about Soviet actions in Cuba and Germany. In 1961, the Soviet Union constructed a wall dividing East and West Berlin, which tore many families apart.

Americans mourned the assassinations of three beloved leaders: President John F. Kennedy, his brother Robert, who was running for the Democratic nomination in 1968, and civil rights leader Martin Luther King Jr. Two attempts were made on President Ford's life.

Civil rights and the Vietnam War were issues that sparked violence. President Johnson signed two acts to provide black Americans with greater equality and rights. To deal with the increasingly unpopular Vietnam War (1959–1975), President Richard Nixon signed a peace treaty in 1973. President Ford declared the war officially over in 1975.

- - - - - **1960** - - - - -

In September, Democratic Senator John F. Kennedy and Republican Vice President Richard M. Nixon face off in a televised **debate**. It's the first time in American history that two presidential candidates debate each other on television. Kennedy narrowly edges Nixon in the popular vote (by just 0.2 percent) but picks up 56 percent of the electoral vote. Kennedy becomes the first Catholic president and the youngest president at age 43. This is the first election in which Alaska and Hawaii, the 49th and 50th states, participate.

On November 22, 1963, Lee Harvey Oswald assassinates Kennedy in Dallas, Texas. Vice President Lyndon Johnson is sworn into office.

John F. Kennedy

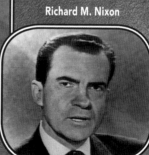

Richard M. Nixon

- - - - - 1964 - - - - -

Johnson runs against Republican Senator Barry Goldwater, whose campaign produces fear of **nuclear war**. Johnson believes that the federal government should support civil rights and social welfare programs. Goldwater does not. Johnson wins in a landslide. At Johnson's urging, Congress passes Civil Rights Acts in 1964 and 1968 to fight against racial **discrimination**. He also wages war on poverty. As a result of his Medicare and Medicaid programs, senior citizens and the poor can receive health insurance.

President Johnson shakes the hand of civil rights leader Martin Luther King Jr. after signing the Civil Rights Act in 1964.

- - - - - 1968 - - - - -

Johnson does not seek re-election. After the assassination of Robert Kennedy in June 1968, the Democrats nominate Hubert Humphrey, Johnson's vice president, to battle Republican candidate Richard Nixon. The campaign season is characterized by anti-war protests, race riots, and assassinations. Nixon squeezes past Humphrey to win the election. Later he stuns the world with his plan to establish relations with Communist China. His trip there in February 1972 is a **diplomatic** success.

President Nixon meets with China's Communist leader, Mao Tse-Tung.

debate—to politely discuss something people disagree about
nuclear war—a war that involves destructive nuclear, or atomic, weapons
discrimination—treating people unfairly because of their race, country of birth, or gender
diplomatic—good at dealing with people

Gerald Ford (left) takes the oath of office to become the 38th president of the United States.

Democratic nominee George McGovern charges that the Nixon administration is the most corrupt in U.S. history. Even so, Nixon wins re-election in a landslide with nearly 18 million more popular votes than McGovern.

But the Nixon administration soon begins to fall apart. On October 10, 1973, Vice President Spiro Agnew resigns when he is charged with not paying his income taxes. Nixon appoints House Minority Leader Gerald Ford as the new vice president. Then on August 8, 1974, Nixon resigns from the presidency as a result of the Watergate scandal. Ford suddenly finds himself president without ever being nominated or elected.

Watergate

In June 1972, five men broke into Democratic National Committee headquarters at the Watergate office building in Washington, D.C. While there, they photographed documents and installed secret listening devices. President Nixon denied any involvement, but *Washington Post* reporters didn't take his word for it. Their investigations revealed taped conversations that proved Nixon was involved in the cover-up plot. But investigators and the FBI were unable to prove that he had ordered the break-in.

Nixon was forced to turn over the tapes to a special committee. Impeachment proceedings began in July 1974. Nixon resigned from the presidency on August 8. The following month, President Ford pardoned him of any crime.

Richard Nixon waves good-bye as he leaves the White House following his resignation.

1976

Americans are fed up with political scandals. Democratic presidential candidate Jimmy Carter promises honesty and a fresh start. He beats Ford in a close election, defeating him by just 2 percent of the popular vote. In November 1979, terrorists take 66 Americans hostage in Iran. Carter sends soldiers to rescue the hostages when other options fail.

Jimmy Carter (left) battles Gerald Ford (right) in a presidential debate.

CHAPTER 9

THE END OF THE 20TH CENTURY (1980-1996)

In the final 20 years of the 20th century, the world stage shifted. The Cold War ended, and Ronald Reagan introduced his own brand of economics. Known as "Reaganomics," this program was meant to give Americans more money in their pockets. But it also greatly increased the national debt.

In the early 1990s, conflicts in the Middle East drew U.S. attention. On January 16, 1991, President George H. W. Bush declared war on Iraq. President Bill Clinton wiped out the astronomical national debt left by Reagan and Bush. His time in office was also characterized by lower **inflation** and decreased crime rates and unemployment. Even so, the media focused on his personal flaws.

At 68 years old, Ronald Reagan was the oldest person ever sworn in as U.S. president.

1980

President Carter takes daring actions to rescue the American hostages in Iran, but they fail miserably. Planes crash, soldiers die, and in the end, Carter's days in the White House are numbered. In televised debates, he is no match for former actor Ronald Reagan, California's Republican governor. They argue about Reagan's desire to take a tough stance with the Soviet Union. Reagan challenges viewers: "Are you better off than you were four years ago?" With an overwhelming 91 percent of the electoral votes, Reagan becomes the oldest U.S. president at the time of his inauguration. In 1981, he survives an attempted assassination, taking a bullet in his left lung.

Fifty-two Americans were held captive in Iran for 444 days. Fourteen of the hostages had been released earlier.

1984

Facing a rebounding economy, Reagan is practically assured re-election. Nicknamed the "Great Communicator," he effectively uses television to promote his policies. He runs against Jimmy Carter's vice president, Walter Mondale, who chooses U.S. Representative Geraldine Ferraro as his running mate. Ferraro is the first woman to run for vice president on a major-party ticket. Reagan's 525 electoral votes (to Mondale's 13) is the most received by a candidate in any U.S. presidential election.

Walter Mondale and Geraldine Ferraro at the 1984 Democratic National Convention in San Francisco

inflation—an increase in prices

- - - - - 1988 - - - - -

The Republican nomination for president goes to Vice President George H. W. Bush. He promises American voters, "Read my lips, no new taxes!" He runs against Michael Dukakis, the Democratic governor of Massachusetts, in one of the most negative campaigns in U.S. history. Bush wins, becoming the first incumbent vice president elected president since Martin Van Buren. In January 1991, Bush orders Operation Desert Storm against Iraq to free Kuwait from Iraqi control.

George H. W. Bush   Michael Dukakis

A U.S. Navy fighter plane flies over burning oil wells in Kuwait during Operation Desert Storm.

The Cold War Ends

In 1987 Ronald Reagan strongly urged Soviet leader Mikhail Gorbachev to tear down the Berlin Wall. Gorbachev announced the end of the Cold War in December 1988. Several dramatic events followed: The Berlin Wall fell in November 1989. East and West Germany reunited in October 1990. And the Soviet Union dissolved into independent nations in the fall of 1991.

German citizens knock down the Berlin Wall.

Bill Clinton gained popularity with young voters when he played saxophone on a late-night talk show. Here he plays again at his inauguration party.

- - - - - 1992 - - - - -

Bush runs for a second term, and early estimates assure his re-election. But self-made billionaire and third-party candidate Ross Perot enters the race and poaches votes from the Republicans. Bill Clinton, the 46-year-old Democratic governor of Arkansas, campaigns for change. The win goes to the youthful and charming Clinton, who is the first "baby boomer" president, meaning he was born between 1946 and 1964.

- - - - - 1996 - - - - -

A booming economy helps President Clinton brush aside allegations of scandal. He wins re-election against Republican Bob Dole of Kansas and Independent candidate Ross Perot. However, in late 1998, Congress votes to impeach Clinton for lying while under oath to tell the truth. Two months later, Congress finds him not guilty of the charges.

CHAPTER 10

THE NEW MILLENNIUM (2000-2012)

On September 11, 2001, terrorists attacked the World Trade Center in New York City and the Pentagon in Washington, D.C., killing thousands. In response, President George W. Bush declared war on terrorism. Americans mobilized for war against Afghanistan and Iraq.

Just as President George W. Bush left office, the U.S. economy faced its most severe **recession** since the Great Depression. Affordable health care had been a hotly debated issue since the Clinton administration. But when Congress passed the Affordable Health Care Act promoted by President Barack Obama, it received mixed reviews.

The Twin Towers of the World Trade Center burn after the terrorist attacks on September 11, 2001.

recession—a temporary slowing of business activity

- - - - - 2000 - - - - -

Al Gore, Clinton's vice president, wins 48.4 percent of the popular vote to 47.9 percent for Texas Governor George W. Bush. At first the media announces Gore as the new president. But then, when it appears Bush has won Florida, he is declared the winner. Because Bush wins Florida by less than 2,000 popular votes, state law requires that the votes be recounted by hand. After the recount, Bush is ahead in Florida by only 327 votes. Democrats demand that the votes in four Florida counties be recounted—again—by hand. This becomes the most controversial presidential election since 1876.

For weeks, the nation waits for an answer while Florida conducts the recounts. The case eventually goes to the Supreme Court, which votes 5–4 to stop the second recount. George W. Bush wins by just five electoral votes.

ELECTORAL VOTE	POPULAR VOTE
 **271**	George W. Bush **47.9%**
 **266**	Al Gore **48.4%**

- - - - - 2004 - - - - -

George W. Bush seeks re-election. He assures Americans that the invasion of Iraq has made the world safer from terrorism. He wins in a close race against Senator John Kerry of Massachusetts.

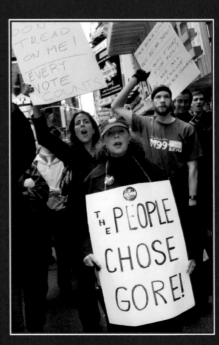

Al Gore supporters rally in support of a recount following the election of 2000.

2008

The Democrats nominate Barack Obama, an African-American U.S. senator from Illinois. Obama is the first black candidate on the ballot in a presidential election in U.S. history.

The Republicans nominate John McCain and his running mate, Alaska Governor Sarah Palin. She is the first female candidate the party has ever put forth on a presidential ballot.

Obama wins easily with more than twice as many electoral votes as McCain. Obama's inauguration draws the largest crowd of any presidential inauguration in U.S. history.

Barack Obama

With more than one million people in attendance, Barack Obama's inauguration was the largest event in the history of Washington, D.C.

- - - - - 2012 - - - - -

Obama effectively uses social media and the Internet to his advantage as he seeks re-election. His strategy is hard to beat, and he easily defeats Republican opponent Mitt Romney in the electoral vote. However, he wins the popular vote by only a 3.8 percent margin.

America has come a long way in its views and actions about the presidency. In the 18th century, the nation's first presidents owned slaves. In the 21st century, a black man became a two-term president. What does the future hold for the American presidency? That remains to be seen. Former First Lady Hillary Clinton will make a bid in 2016 to become the first female president of the United States.

I'm with Hillary
hillaryclinton.com

GLOSSARY

amendment (uh-MEND-muhnt)—a change made to a law or a legal document

assassination (uh-sass-uh-NAY-shun)—the murder of someone who is well known or important

Cold War (KOHLD WOR)—a conflict between the United States and the Soviet Union; although there was no direct fighting, the conflict lasted from about 1947 to 1990

communism (KAHM-yuh-ni-zuhm)—a way of running a country in which the government owns almost everything

Constitutional Convention of 1787 (kon-stuh-TOO-shuh-nuhl kuhn-VEN-shuhn)— a gathering in which representatives of the United States developed laws by which the new country would govern itself

corruption (kuh-RUP-shuhn)—doing things that are wrong or illegal to get money, favors, or power

debate (di-BATE)—to politely discuss something people disagree about

diplomatic (di-pluh-MA-tik)—good at dealing with people

discrimination (dis-kri-muh-NAY-shuhn)— treating people unfairly because of their race, country of birth, or gender

electors (ee-LEHK-tohrz)—people who vote to choose between candidates running for office

impeach (im-PEECH)—to bring formal charges against a public official who may have committed a crime while in office

inauguration (in-aw-gyuh-RAY-shuhn)—a formal ceremony to swear a person into political office

incumbent (in-KUM-bent)—the person currently in office

inflation (in-FLAY-shuhn)—an increase in prices

monopoly (muh-NOP-uh-lee)—a situation in which a supplier can control the price of a good or service because it is the only supplier

neutral (NOO-truhl)—not taking any side in a war

nominate (NOM-uh-nate)—to suggest that someone would be the right person to do a job

nonconsecutive (NON-kuhn-SEK-yuh-tiv)— with a gap between; not one after the other

pneumonia (noo-MOH-nyuh)—a serious disease that causes the lungs to become inflamed and filled with fluid, which makes breathing difficult

polio (POH-lee-oh)—a disease affecting the nerves, spinal cord, and brain

primary (PRYE-mair-ee)—an election in which candidates of the same party try to win the party's nomination as candidate for a particular office

profiteer (PROF-i-teer)—to make money by selling goods that are in short supply

recession (ri-SESH-uhn)—a temporary slowing of business activity

repeal (ri-PEEL)—to officially cancel something, such as a law

resign (ri-ZINE)—to voluntarily give up a job, position, or office

running mate (RUHN-ning MATE)—the person a candidate is running with

secede (si-SEED)—to formally withdraw from a group or an organization, often to form another organization

speakeasy (SPEEK-ee-zee)—a place that illegally sells alcoholic drinks

superpower (SOO-pur-pou-ur)—an extremely powerful nation

unanimously (yoo-NAN-uh-muhss-lee)— agreed on by everyone

READ MORE

Davis, Todd, and Marc Frey. *The New Big Book of U.S. Presidents.* Philadelphia: Running Press Kids, 2013.

Jackson, Carolyn. *The Election Book: The People Pick a President.* New York: Scholastic, 2012.

Sobel, Syl. *Presidential Elections and Other Cool Facts.* Hauppauge, N.Y.: Barron's, 2012.

Townsend, Michael. *Where Do Presidents Come From?: And Other Presidential Stuff of Super Great Importance.* New York: Dial Books for Young Readers, 2012.

CRITICAL THINKING USING THE COMMON CORE

1. The 25th Amendment did not pass until 1967, nearly 200 years after the Constitution went into effect. Explain what the 25th Amendment says. If the 25th Amendment had been in effect 100 years earlier, how might that have changed history? (Key Ideas and Details)

2. Do you think the Electoral College is a fair system for electing a president? Why or why not? Use examples from the text to support your answer. (Integration of Knowledge and Ideas)

3. The election of 2000 was particularly controversial and could have easily resulted in a different outcome. Explain what happened in that election. What would have been the outcome if the election was decided by the popular vote rather than the Electoral College? (Integration of Knowledge and Ideas)

INDEX

INTERNET SITES

FactHound offers a safe, fun way to find Internet sites related to this book.
All of the sites on FactHound have been researched by our staff.

Here's all you do:
Visit *www.facthound.com*
Type in this code: 9781491482391